THINK LIKE A KING, ACT LIKE A KING

The Proverbs 31 Man

A Celebration of Men &

Those Who Love Them

PUBLISHER

All rights reserved. No part of this book may be reproduced in any form without permission in writing from the publisher, except in the case of brief quotations embodied in critical articles or reviews.

ISBN

978-0-692-73874-0

Cover & Interior Design: Nicole Young Starks
Photo credit: Paul Best Photography

Also available as an eBook at www.amazon.com

Printed in the United States of America

www.victoriouslynicole.com

Dedication

My first published book is dedicated to all of the kings in my life,
First, the King of Kings, my Jesus Christ, Lord, Savior, Best Friend, Lover, my Everything-my life is NOTHING without you.
To the king who God used to create me, my father, Henry C. Young, Sr.-I honor you. May God bless and keep you always!
To the first king that I really knew and loved, my brother, Henry C. Young, Jr. - I am excited about your journey and how you are beginning to reign. Thank you for being Genesis' and Mercy's
first love!

To my one and only nephew, Braylen Joshua – you are indeed a prince evolving into a king. You are so intelligent, talented, and loving. It is because of you that I have written this book. My prayer is that you will overcome every challenge in your life to become the king you were destined to be. I love you Braylen Joshua!
Make "Ti-Ti" proud!

Finally, to Phillip Michael- Thank you for giving me insight
of a king's life.

In memory of the kings in my life who have left us,
but who are not forgotten:
Henry Jefferson Young, Amos Jones, Richard Young, Bishop Joseph D. Farris, Robert Young, and Oprather Johnson

The Inspiration Behind the Book
Proverbs 31:1-9

The words of King Lemuel, the utterance which his mother taught him:
2 What, my son?
And what, son of my womb?
And what, son of my vows?
3 Do not give your strength to women,
Nor your ways to that which destroys kings.
4 It is not for kings, O Lemuel,
It is not for kings to drink wine,
Nor for princes intoxicating drink;
5 Lest they drink and forget the law,
And pervert the justice of all the afflicted.
6 Give strong drink to him who is perishing,
And wine to those who are bitter of heart.
7 Let him drink and forget his poverty,
And remember his misery no more.
8 Open your mouth for the speechless,
In the cause of all who are appointed to die.
9 Open your mouth, judge righteously,
And plead the cause of the poor and needy.

Contents

CONTENTS ....

Chapter One 13
   YOU WERE BORN TO BE A KING 13

Chapter Two 20
   KINGS ARE FOR KINGDOMS 20

Chapter 3 35
   THE FALLEN KING 35

Chapter 4 45
   KING OF HEARTS 45

Chapter 5 62
   ALL THE KING'S HORSES 62

Chapter 6 70
   ALL THE KING'S MEN 70

Chapter 7 88
   "KING ME" 88

FINAL WORDS 102

MEET THE AUTHOR 105

THINK LIKE A KING, ACT LIKE A KING
The Proverbs 31 Man

INTRODUCTION

Have you discovered yet, that God has an enormous sense of humor? Why wouldn't He? He is the source for every living thing. ***"It is in Him that I live, breath and have my being." * Acts 17:28.** God has always desired to have a very close and intimate relationship with His children. As a result, He is in tune with every part of us and I am deeply convinced that God has a sense of humor.

With this in mind, I find it very funny that after working with women nearly 20 years, professionally and in ministry that my very first book would be written to MEN!! Even now, as I am writing this I am shaking my head. However, it is not that farfetched. I have been blessed to work with several women and their families as a home based counselor and case manager. In my work, I heard many stories and witnessed several areas of emptiness because there was a lack of positive, male role models.

Also, being a woman provides me a strong platform in which to discuss what women are looking for in men. Not just romantically, but what daughters are looking for in fathers and what mothers are hoping for their sons to become. The universe is fulfilled when men are living the very essence of who there were created to be. It was after reading King Lemuel's mother's message to him in Proverbs 31:1-9, that I was deeply inspired to write my own message to men.

For centuries, we have celebrated the *"Virtuous Woman"*, also known as *"The Proverbs 31 Woman"*. It was so refreshing to see a new and not so celebrated view of the PROVERBS 31 MAN! Seeing God's humor happened again when I shared with others the title of this book.

Some attempted to clarify for me that there was *not* a Proverbs 31 Man. A kiddish smile would appear as I "corrected" *them* and with excitement referred them back to the chapter, this time advising them to pay special attention to verses 1-9. In fact, this occurred while attending a very special fundraiser dinner, honoring the life of a king who had served our community and had recently died. My gracious hostess excitedly announced that I was writing a book and proceeded in asking me to share it with the others at the table. When I did, one lovely lady challenged me and doubted whether the passage referred to women and not men.

Again, with that same kiddish look, I happily referred her to the first 9 verses. Everyone at the table looked in shock to learn that this was a possibility. From the side of my eye, I saw the lady immediately go to her IPhone. I wondered if she was checking this fact on Google for herself. I was not offended

about any of those challenges. Instead, I was encouraged that I was doing the right thing. All of this just confirmed the sentiments of my heart that God's Word did not leave out the existence of a virtuous man. Spiritually speaking, the strength and wisdom of women have been celebrated for centuries. What about the men? In spite of what media projects, I still believe that good men exist. For me to say this, is mostly a declaration of faith because I did not grow up feeling this way. As a child, most of the strongest male role models in my life died when I was too young to understand the impact of not having them.

My grandfather, Henry Jefferson Young, was the first model of a strong, honorable and God fearing man. He was a basketball state champion at Muncie High School. He was a military man who married and took great care of his wife and children. Working for the U. S. Postal Service, he provided a comfortable and financially stable household- in a middle class neighborhood, which was not as common for African Americans as it is today. Standing nearly 7ft, he was the tallest deacon at Zion Tabernacle Apostolic Church.

Consistently, I could depend on him each week, after Sunday School, to open the soda machine and get me and my friends a can of "Sunkist" pop. This made me so proud and I felt so very special. I also saw him as king because during sleepovers at my grandparents' house, his work ethic and discipline was so evident. Even after his retirement, every morning at the crack of dawn, the house would wake up to the wonderful smell of bacon, toast, and coffee. To this day, I have him to thank for my devotion to Starbucks. When he died from brain cancer, I was devastated!

Not too far away from that, my grandfather Amos had died as well. The evil "D" had already happened in my family. Divorce came to place a wedge between me and my father. Although I believe he loved me, the separation and absence communicated to me that he didn't.

Aside from my uncles, who lived out of town, there weren't many more good men to look up to. It would be several years for me to find that kind of role model again. You see, I have had a wealth of great female role models in my life. I have wonderful aunts, cousins, and friends who demonstrate love, strength, and virtue.

The matriarch in my family, Beatrice Louise Johnson Jones, is someone to be reckoned. It would not be fair to introduce you to her here because her legacy deserves her having an entire book, and it is soon to come! I will briefly conclude that to know this remarkable woman is pure bliss, there will never be another woman like her! Then to have been blessed with the treasure of my mother, Jarline Williams Young, is added evidence of the Proverbs 31 women in my life. Amidst the sacrifices and struggles, she raised three children, went back to college to obtain a Bachelor's and Master's degree and provided a quality life for her family.

It was her strong faith in God and determination that evicted us from public housing and removed our family from government assistance. I am confident that my strong faith, resolve for community service and conviction to make a difference, has come from her. She, too, is deserving of her own book.

When it came to having strong male role models, my world view had been biased. Throughout my life, I had longed to have the same strong, positive presence of men. As a result, I began to pray and seek for a better understanding of men and to learn God's intent for them in society and in faith. This journey evolved into me having a greater appreciation and celebration of one of God's prized creation, **men**!

Along this journey, I have observed that a good woman is the perfect complement to a good man. A woman's qualities are intended to intertwine with the man's, to produce balance, harmony, and, completeness. So, naturally when either one of them is out of place, there will be completely opposite outcomes of imbalance, discord, and lack. God never intended for this to be the case. In the pages ahead you will see God's magnificent plan displayed as He shared it with me.

My prayer is that men and women will be inspired to evaluate their purpose and how it can be a compliment to each other. God's creation of man and woman transcends gender. This book is not to debate this because God has already provided us the master plan for that. It is not my assignment to rehash and regurgitate the current debate about gender issues. However, God's download to me may challenge views on this social and moral issue. When a man is aligned with their Creator's plan, *every* facet of that man will be in order. After reading this devotional, my prayer is that men will claim their inheritance as a king. As a result they will be empowered to make a positive impact in their families, communities, and churches.

Likewise, I hope that the queens in their lives will have a deeper appreciation and burden to support them in their newly or reclaimed role. Together, the kings and queens will reflect God's true love for mankind, ultimately demonstrating virtuous men *and* women!

Chapter One

YOU WERE BORN TO BE A KING

Dear Your Highness,

Did you know that you were a king? So what, you weren't born with a silver spoon in your mouth or you did not live in the wealthiest of neighborhoods. Your biological pedigree may appear to be far from royalty, but the reality is that you were created to be a bona fide king. I apologize that you may not have had this understanding before. For sure, knowing your identity could have prevented you from making poor decisions in the past.

Possibly, your life path could have been more pleasurable and productive. Without further ado, I would like to introduce you to yourself as the king you were created to be.

I have always been fascinated with fairy tales. Who doesn't want to experience utopia, and live in a world of perfection and harmony? The increased popularity of Yoga and meditation is visible proof of that. However, you don't have to live long to realize that life is not a fairy tale.

If you are fortunate, you may have experienced moments of euphoric bliss, but it does not last forever. If you are hopeless romantic like me, you do not have to feel bad for appreciating a good fairy tale or two. In fact, the concept of utopia actually began with God.

My evidence to support this concept can be found in the beginning of time. God masterfully created the heavens and the earth. After 5 glorious days, once upon a time, in the beginning of time, on what we would call a Friday- God saw His majestic creation of the world and felt it was incomplete. To fulfill this
void, He created a masterpiece, a *MAN*! To further enhance this masterpiece, a *woMAN* was formed from this man.

In this real story, God created a kingdom full of beauty and bliss. Everything was perfect. King Adam did not have a need for anything. I imagine everyday was a sunny day, the perfect temperature of 73 degrees, no humidity with a cool breeze blowing in Eve's hair, but I'm not the author of that story. To top it all off, King Adam was gifted the most beautiful woman to share his kingdom. Queen Eve was born flawless with no need for cosmetic enhancements. She did not need liposuction, Botox, or hair extensions, she was perfect for her king. Together, they were both the expressed image of their creator, the Almighty God.

Can you imagine a kingdom where all of your needs are supplied? In this paradise, there were plenty of delicacies to eat, not just mundane food. The king and queen were in perfect
health. They had a perfect and passionate love where they could read each other's minds because they had the same mind. They were truly one entity. Quarrels and bickering did not exist. Queen Eve did not have to wonder where Adam was or who he was with. Infidelity was nonexistent because there were no others to be tempted. Resources were plenteous and there was no need to worry about bills, savings, and retirement. Just imagine a place of perfect worship without distractions. The wondrous creation was in concert worshipping their Creator, Father God.

When considering God's plan for men, my heart was saddened and my spirit was disturbed when I observed the current state of manhood. I was raised in the church, a true pew baby. In my walk with the Lord, I vividly recall the consistent encouragement for the women of faith to aspire to be a "Proverbs 31 Woman. Initially, such an accomplishment seemed nearly impossible! Yet, every year on "Women's Day" there was a campaign to recruit more super women.

I cannot tell you how many times I've read this passage in Sunday School, Bible Study, Vacation Bible School, my own personal Bible study and more.

Becoming a Proverbs 31 Woman has been a lifelong aspiration and it will take a lifetime to accomplish. In truth, this portrait of a virtuous woman is very honorable. Although I have not mastered it all, I do believe that it *is* possible to possess all the virtuous attributes throughout a lifetime, when done in the Holy Spirit. Seriously, we cannot do it without God's spirit. Some would say that I stumbled upon the Proverbs 31 Man. In contrary, I know it was divine intervention.

How is it that I had grown up in the faith and not noticed that the first 9 verses were actually addressed to men! It was a lightbulb moment: Proverbs 31 was not just for women!
In fact, the chapter opens with a king's mother instructing him and giving him wise counsel to be a VIRTUOUS MAN!!!!! Why hasn't this been celebrated on Men's Day? But I digress. As it relates to today, this mother

spoke to the *king* of a man. Really, I should not have been so shocked because God is an equal opportunity creator. God's love and equality for women can be seen throughout the Bible. Inequality has always been mankind's agenda. It is the sinful nature that makes differences in the value of men and women. Before their "fall", Adam and Eve were created with the same value and worth.

Going back, God's plan for Adam and for you is to reign as king. ***And ye shall be unto me a kingdom of priests, and an holy nation. These are the words which thou shalt speak unto the children of Israel. (Exodus 19:6)***

It was always intended for you to live a privileged life where every aspect of your life is fulfilled. You were created in God's image and for His glory. With every breath that is taken, you demonstrate His masterpiece because He breathed the breath of life in you and you became a living soul (Genesis 2:7).

In the pages to come, I pray that you will be challenged to improve, motivated to change, and inspired to succeed as the king you were created to be!

Dear Father, God,

Your plan for the Kingdom is beyond comprehension. I am amazed at your creativity. The heavens and earth declare your glory. All that is within them continue to show forth your praise. Yet, it was not until you formed King Adam that you braggadociously declared that he was your greatest creation. His queen only further enhanced your plan.

Many dispensations have passed since the creation of King Adam. However, your plan was always intended to transcend time and space.

Even today, each man is equipped to be the king you created him to be. They possesses the ability to function above earthly existence. Father, I pray that you will impress upon the king's heart to assume his special role, not settling to be anything less. Father, allow the pages in this book to serve as a mirror reflection of your intent for his life. In Jesus Christ's Name, amen.

Chapter Two

KINGS ARE FOR KINGDOMS

Dear Your Highness,

So now that you have been introduced to yourself as king, are you aware of all of the benefits that you have in your newly assumed role? In your role as king, you have inherited dominion power, and rule! Wow! Yes, you can poke your chest out a little and feel special because you were chosen to reign. God's Word says: **"behold, the kingdom of God is within you." Luke 17:21** In part, consider this chapter as the orientation that you would receive on a new job. Your new employer would first welcome you to the company and tell you of all of the wonderful things that makes it great. It's to reassure you that you have made the right decision working there.

Next, they will provide you with an overview of how the company operates. You know, the "what to dos" and what not to dos". Lastly, they explain to you your benefit package. Inclued can be health insurance, life insurance, vacation time, and 401k, if you are blessed and fortunate.

Regarding your search for fulfillment, I know that you have spent a lifetime trying to find your place. You've spent time, energy, and a lot of money to secure your status, not knowing that you had the power all along. With your newly found identity, now you can take your place in the kingdom.

The Kingdom of God is where He resides, rules, and reigns-it is His holy domain. Love, joy, and peace exists there, but it is also where His governance and ruling is displayed. Just as any employer would have policies, so does God for His kingdom. The Holy Bible is God's Employee Handbook. I can recall times at work where I would ask a coworker a question.

Sometimes they would answer the question. If their patience wore out, they would refer me back to the "Employee Handbook". You have that same resource. If you desire to know how to conduct yourself in the kingdom, I am referring you back to the Bible. There are 66 books that are full of instructions, advice, and encouragement to help you in your life.

God's kingdom is royal. Have you ever watched a royal event on television or any type of social media? My fondest memory and first glimpse of what royalty looked like was waking up early in the morning to watch Prince Charles and Lady Diana's Royal Wedding. It was the premier event of the year, no matter where in the world you lived.

I was not the only one captivated as nearly 17 million Americans alone, tuned in to watch. While so many snub royal activities, there is something so captivating about it to me. It is simply fascinating watching the protocol and the prestigious
formalities. Everyone from the guards to the adjutants know their role. They are very prepared and confident. Likewise, the royals behave in a manner that demands respect and attention. Why do you think this is so? Because everyone involved has a clear sense of their identity. From birth, royals have been groomed and instructed on how to conduct themselves. Never do they second guess their roles. They conduct themselves accordingly because they are fully aware of their power and responsibilities.

The importance of assuming your role in the kingdom is crucial. First, when you reign, God is glorified as your creator. *"**But ye are a chosen generation, a royal priesthood, an holy nation, a peculiar*** *people; that ye should shew forth the praises of him who hath called you out of darkness into his marvellous light,"* I Peter 2:9

In the United States, it may be challenging to truly understand the concept of royalty because our country is a democracy. President Barack Obama would be the closest example of a king for the U.S. Whether you appreciate him or not, he is highly esteemed and honored with other nation's rulers because of his role as President.

However, his power is still limited because the United States is not a monarchy. Mostly, President Obama's decisions and actions are in collaboration with his cabinet, the Senate, the House of Representatives, and the Supreme Court. In your life, the King of Kings is who you answer to and He has given you power and permission to live with dominion.

Have you thought about what your life would look like if you lived in dominion? First, after you are born again of the Spirit, God has provided you His Dunamis power, which literally means explosive power (Acts 1:8).

With this power sin has no dominion over you. This same power can then be evident in every part of your life and will blow your mind and enable you to do amazing things in your life (Ephesians 3:20). This, the original super power, can assist you in overcoming every obstacle and challenge in your life.

God's kingdom has order. Recently, I was blessed with the opportunity to participate in my first global mission trip to Haiti. Geographically, it is natural for the temperature to be extremely hot. However, I learned from our local tour guide that due to the cutting down of the trees for commerce, the country experienced even hotter weather because there were not enough trees to provide cooling. Somehow, not having vegetation hindered rainfall, which decreased the growth in trees! It seemed like a vicious cycle-less trees, resulted in less rain, which resulted in less trees. My global mission team completed a great deal of the work out in the blazing sun.

We were ever grateful whenever we could find relief under a tree. It was like playing musical chairs because when someone moved, there was someone eagerly waiting to take their spot just to cool off.

Having order in the kingdom provides comfort and protection. When one element is out of place the rest will be out of order. God was not confused when he created the family to include the father, mother, and children. It sounds so "old fashioned" today. But this is not to be debated if you are a follower of Jesus Christ. Realistically, every family will not look the same because of death, divorce, and other causes. Ultimately, it is still the sinful nature that is to blame for them all. God's family order is His ultimate desire and plan for wholeness.

It is vital that kings return to their position in the family. Our society is reaping the consequence of kings not

being good husbands and good fathers. Just as cutting down trees in certain parts of the world can disrupt the ecosystem and environment, so it is when the family is disrupted as a result of you not answering the call to being a strong foundation for your family.

My burden for families of divorce comes from my own family background. It is sad how divorce shreds families apart. However, I will not use this book as a platform to hurt family members. Instead, my goal is to expose the spirit behind divorce and to provide insight on its impact on families and society as a whole. As a Christian, I have resolved to forgive and I die daily to forgiveness. It's not always easy, but it is possible.

I love my father and mother and instead of hating them, I detest the enemy that pulled them apart.

I will share with you that I often wonder how my life would have been different had my family been whole with two parents. At times I have spent moments daydreaming about what my personal choices would have been, had I consistently heard affirmations from my king: *"Nicki, you can do it"*, *"I believe in you"*, *"You are beautiful just the way you are"*, *"Don't do that"*.... What I do know for sure is that when I met the King of Kings at the age of 7 years old, it was a like a lifeguard rescuing me from drowning in the ocean. You see, I was born again and this began my walk with my Heavenly *Father*, Jesus Christ.

This was a major turning point in life and I can only imagine that my life would have been a tragedy without Him. Where I did not get the affirmations, I received them from my Heavenly Father and His love letters to me from the Bible. It was then that I clung to the scripture that says when **"my father and mother forsake me, then the Lord will take me up."** (Psalm 27:10). I have found Jesus to be my superhero and the happy ending to my story.

I acknowledge that I was set up to fail and to fall into the stereotypical patterns that exist for girls who are not raised with a father. My personal testimony is that my relationship with Jesus Christ gave me self-confidence and self-esteem. As a result, I escaped teen pregnancy, dropping out of high school, experiencing drugs, and the list of other statistics that are associated with fatherless girls. I am not alone, there are many women who have escaped differently, but this is *my* testimony.

Also, it is important for me to share with you that God has provided me tremendous love and this love allows me to forgive.

With joy, I can announce that I am no longer bitter, but *better*! However, this book would not be complete or authentic without me including my plea to husbands and fathers. If you believe that you can reign and that your life can be complete without doing right by your family, you are sadly mistaken.

Furthermore, you are not reigning if your family is broken and dysfunctional due to your absence of being a Godly husband and father.

The family is a beautiful reflection of God's love for His children. Just as we can depend on Him to love, care for, provide, and protect us, the same applies to husbands and fathers. As the husband, you are encouraged and expected to love your wife like Christ loves the church. ***"Husbands, love your wives, even as Christ also loved the church, and gave himself for it;"* Ephesians 5:25**

At times it may be a sacrifice to love your wife, and this is correct- it is a huge sacrifice. But you chose her to be your wife and you made that commitment before God and witnesses. Today, we live in a selfish society and it's *"every man for themselves"*. The vows did not make provision for you to forsake your wife because you no longer love her anymore, or she gained a few more pounds, or turned out to be evil.

For these and other reasons, there are resources to help you rediscover why you married your wife in the beginning. Take advantage of Christian counseling or meet with your pastor. So many people invest money in far less valuable things than their family. If you desire to demonstrate power within your family, it is essential that you work to maintain it. Anything worth having is worth working for.

Are you aware that you have dethroned yourself each time your wife is disrespected, abandoned and mistreated? With exception to abuse or deeper areas of mistrust, do whatever it takes to fight for your marriage. Just know that if you choose not to do so, this is not pleasing to God and you are living beneath your reign. This kind of irresponsibility is offensive to God and the repercussions can be found in so many other areas of your life, especially in your family. From a queen's perspective, we love to be cherished and lavished with attention, love and security. Even more, it is honorable when a man takes responsibility and takes care of his children, making his family top priority. There is nothing more attractive to a queen than a king who possesses these qualities.

As I have said before, God is an equal opportunity creator. The wife has a role to play in this as well. In the same chapter of Ephesians 5, wives are instructed to honor their husbands. However, being the king of your castle demands a king who is honorable and noble. By doing this you are setting a good example for your children.

In fatherhood, your role is more than paying the bills and providing the family's needs. While this is expected and the right thing to do, it is not the only role that you play in their life. Your children need your undivided attention and quality time. They also need guidance and instruction. ***"Train up a child in the way he should go: and when he is old, he will***

 ***not depart from it."* Proverbs 22:6.** Remember, you are the expressed image of God.

Just like He can be a provider, protector, friend, and more, He has given you the ability to serve your family in the same way. As the king of your family, your children need to hear you speak destiny into their lives. Do not allow the world to shape their identity and eventually, their destiny. You have the responsibility to raise future kings and queens for not just your kingdom, but more importantly for the Kingdom of God.

God's original plan for mothers never included raising children alone. Single mothers as parents is an epidemic today. Because of the father's absence, mothers are forced to be the *breadwinners, disciplinarians, nurturers, housekeepers, parole officers, nurses,* and so much more for their children. It's no wonder why so many single mothers are attacked with cancer, diabetes, and heart disease. Sure, a mother can raise children alone. I have seen many do it successfully, but at what cost? It's just not fair and in God's eyes, it is not acceptable!

It is very common for abandoned children to struggle with depression, self-esteem, unnecessary insecurities, fears, and an overall dissatisfaction in life. Fathers, when you leave mothers to raise your son alone, you have employed her without her having the proper skills and qualifications to do the best job. She cannot model the traits of a man because, she is a woman. Your physical absence results in the absence of the base in your voice, your testosterone, and your smelly grime of hard work.

Fatherless children miss out on seeing you working hard to protect your family. They miss out on seeing you arguing with their mother, but then to go back to hug and kiss her, showing them that everything will be ok, even if it is only temporary. Your children deserve to see from you that life is not going to be perfect, but with perseverance, life can be good.

Even more, father-daughter relationships are just as important as father-son relationships. Fathers should be their daughter's first love as it is the first expression of love that they will know. When a father models respect, love, and appreciation for their daughter, she is given a guide to help her in future relationships with males, both romantically and platonically. Did you know fathers that you also build confidence, strength, and tenacity in your daughters? Who wouldn't want to be their daughter's hero? You have that privilege, please use it.

I am the eldest of 3 children and I have only one brother. Although I am older than him, I often call him my "big" brother. Partly because he *is* really much taller than me. But there is something within me that longs to look up to him in admiration. Henry, Jr. has two beautiful girls and every chance I get,
I remind him to be their first love. I often encourage him that if he is not, it will leave room for potential scoundrels to take his place.

It is my mission to speak out and to invoke change. It is my hope that more fathers will step up. For too long we have used and abused the adage: "It takes a village to raise a child." Let's stop using the *"village"* as a backup plan to God's plan. Fathers: raise your own children!

Dear Father, God,

What a delight it is to know that the institution of family is a reflection of your love for us. Your master plan for the Kingdom provides us a handbook for their success. First, forgive those who have fallen short as husbands and fathers. Likewise, give them a conviction in their heart to be obedient to your plan. Father, I am praying for disruption and destruction of whatever allures them away from being the king in their families.

Perhaps they did not know the negative impact of their choices until now. Please allow them to know your grace and that it is not too late to regain their throne. Bring restoration to families as the kings realign themselves to their call and responsibilities. You have equipped each man with power and esteem. When they function in this ability they are at their fullest potential. Lord, I am praying that the amount of broken families will decrease and that whole families will increase. This I pray in your name, Jesus Christ, amen.

Chapter 3
THE FALLEN KING

Dear Your Highness,

For sure the pressure to live up to your calling to rule as king can be overwhelming. Initially, your responsibilities were never intended to cause you to fail or to fall. In the very beginning, all creation was perfect and needed little intervention. Your role was merely to have dominion, not to conquer. At that time, there was nothing to conquer only to rule. However, not far from the beginning of time, a villain surfaced to dethrone man.

When Satan and sin entered into the world, this shifted everything. Now, there was a competition between the devil and man to conquer what God intended to be ruled by man. This power struggle continues today. However, Jesus Christ came to destroy the works of the devil and to redeem you back to your intended rule! (I John 3:8) There is no excuse for you to live in defeat.

Many would be very surprised to know that I, a very feminine and "girly girl", *love* superhero movies just the same as fairy tales. There's nothing like the rush after watching a superhero defeat the villain. Almost always, just like fairy tales, the superhero movies have a happy ending. However, in superhero stories, in order to get to that happy ending there is a lot of drama, pain, and turmoil to overcome.

To continue the story, King Adam and Queen Eve lived in paradise. There was not a need for anything. They were in harmony with God and each other. It was the picture of perfection on all levels. Satan and sin entered and this all changed. A little history on Satan: he was a fallen angel who at one time was the chief musician in heaven. He had a measure of power, but he felt that it was not enough. He wanted to be God instead of a chief angel. It was his arrogance and disrespect for God's authority where he lost his place, initial power, and rule (Isaiah 14:12-15). When Satan saw that King Adam was given dominion, he determined that he would live to dethrone him and all of mankind. Satan knew that the only way King Adam would lose his power was if he could manipulate and trick him into surrendering it and that is exactly what happened.

In the Garden of Eden, Satan deceived Queen Eve into eating from the *Tree of Knowledge of Good and Evil*. This was the ONLY commandment that God gave to them. Aside from that, they were free to do whatever else they wanted to do. Really, Adam and Eve? It was disobeying that very commandment that caused them to fall from dominion and power.

Today, mankind is rippled with the consequences of King Adam and Queen Eve's sin. Sin is defined as the transgression or disobedience to God's law. The consequences of sin is death. ***"For the wages of sin is death; but the gift of God is eternal life through Jesus Christ our Lord."*(Romans 6:23)**

Great news: redemption is available now, but the reality of sin is still present. Sin is the ultimate cause for the ails of this world. When a man is succumbed to sin, he is disabled from being the king he was created to be.

The Bible says we are born in sin and shaped in iniquity (Psalm 51:5). Also, as a result of the Great Fall, all have sinned and fallen short of the glory of God (Romans 3:23). Jesus Christ came to redeem mankind to its rightful place. However, daily men are defeated due to sin. Sin separates us from God. It keeps all us from living the life that God created us to live. The fact is that sin diminishes your power and rule.

Remember the picture of the 73 degree, sunny day with a cool breeze flowing through Eve's hair? Well, figuratively, that had all been interrupted by sin. The script changed and the harmonious relationship between them and God was temporarily deleted. Until fellowship with God is reestablished and maintained, sin will continue to have dominion, power and rule.

Looking back at Adam and Eve, before they sinned, they were free, naked and not ashamed. Their fall from grace left mankind in turmoil and exposed us to the detriment of sin.

In regards to falling, do you remember the nursery rhyme, Humpty Dumpty?

Humpty Dumpty sat on a wall

Humpty Dumpty had a great fall....

The story never said why Humpty Dumpty fell. This leaves it up to the audience to use their imaginations and to draw their own conclusion. Spiritually speaking, Humpty Dumpty had no business on the wall. From my understanding, he was too big to be on the wall, anyway. Sometimes, it is the same with men today.

Regarding sin, many times men have put themselves in places of temptation and it only sets them up to fail. If you are a king, why would you want to live like a pauper or bum? Why would a king be caught in low living? I'm also reminded of the prodigal son (Luke 15) who was born into wealth. His ego and foolishness prompted him to ask his father for his inheritance early and to use it foolishly.

Eventually, he found himself eating the pig's food! Again, I ask: how does royalty find themselves in the pen with pigs? Not having a clear understanding of your identity is a clear way to end up with the filthy swine. Also, not knowing the value of your birthright can cause you to throw it all away for a moment of temporary pleasure.

Now, let's talk about those temporary pleasures. The king's mother in Proverbs 31 was very explicit in advising her son to refrain from activities that would defeat him. She warned him from being drunk in access and being weak to women. I believe that it is a man's nature to be playful and adventurous. From childhood, this innate inclination was strengthened by encouraging you to play to your wit's end. You were celebrated when you played in the mud or fell out of a tree.

Meanwhile, as you were causing ruckus as kids, girls were learning to be responsible by playing "house", pretending to cook, clean, "playing dress up" and caring for plastic baby dolls. Each year, millions of dollars are spent on sports and mostly by men. Professional sports (which is in my opinion institutionalized playtime) is a billion dollar industry. It's not completely your fault that you would rather play, instead of being serious and responsible.

Our society has created this monster, hence the need for the Proverbs 31 Man to rise and takes his place as a king.

For some, our western society has allowed you to be playful and not accept responsibility for too long. For this reason, it is hard for you to adjust and grow up. You may mature physically, but some of you are still little boys stuck in a man's body refusing to grow up.

Some of my fondest childhood memories are from spending the summer in Benton Harbor, Michigan. I can vividly remember my uncles washing their cars, the old fashioned way-by hand. They would have tunes from artists like "Earth, Wind, and Fire" or the "O'Jay's" blasting and there were suds for days! It was like watching an overgrown boy playing with their toys all over again. I strongly believe that life is to be lived and to be lived well. God has provided for us so many pleasures to enjoy.

However, when indulging in behaviors and activities threaten to disrupt your fellowship with God and ruin valuable relationships, it has gone too far.

At some point, you have to grow up. Forsaking your responsibilities is another sure way to be falling. Referring back to the prodigal son, he failed by forsaking his responsibilities to his father and family. His temporary insanity took him further than he anticipated. Taking note, even with King Adam, where was he when Satan tempted Queen Eve? King Adam was to be her covering and protection. How did Satan get enough space of time to beguile Eve? Where in the world was Adam while this was happening? He fell from his position and opened the door for sin to appear.

When a man is consumed with who he is and fulfilling his role in Christ, there is very little time to be tricked by the enemy. You just do not have a whole lot of time to fall. Like the old people used to tell us, *"an idol mind is the devil's workshop"*. What are your idols? What are the activities and interests that have consumed your life? What is invading God's space in your heart and mind? I can guarantee that whatever it is, it will cause you to fall and ultimately fail.

Hopefully, by now you have a clear picture of Satan's agenda for you to fall. However, there is a superhero that can activate His power in your life. God can keep you from falling. ***"Now unto him that is able to keep you from falling, and to present you faultless before the presence of his glory with exceeding joy. To the only wise God our Saviour, be glory and majesty, dominion and power, both now and ever. Amen."*** (Jude 1:25)

I am telling my age, but in the old church, the mother saints used to tell us, *"You can be kept, if you **wanna** be kept!"*

Be encouraged in knowing that if you fall, there is an advocate with the Father who has come to eradicate sin.

"If we confess our sins, he is faithful and just to forgive us our sins, and to cleanse us from all unrighteousness", **I John 1:9**. God has erased all excuses for you not to reign. Now, what is your excuse?

Dear Heavenly Father,

Thank you for giving men the example of King Adam's fall. It is a reminder and warning not to lose focus on their identity and responsibility. Right now, I am lifting up my brothers in prayer. As kings, there is an imminent enemy that has desired to sift them as wheat. Their responsibility to live blameless and without reproach is beyond necessary. I am asking that you enlighten them to count the costs of their decisions and choices.

Lord, please help them to be aware that the enemy's sole purpose is to destroy their soul. Lord, raise their awareness and cause them to be cautious of their potential to fall. Their role as king does not exclude them from temptation, as King Adam was
tempted and fell. May they daily rehearse the prayer that you have taught them to not be led into temptation, but to be delivered from evil. Empower them through your Holy Spirit to overcome every sinful battle in their life. In Jesus Christ's Name, amen.

Chapter 4
KING OF HEARTS

Dear Your Highness,

Now that you have been reminded that you are a king and that you are fully aware of your authority, it is crucial that I talk to you about your heart. Contrary to many beliefs, you do have a big heart and a great capacity to love and conquer. This is often overlooked and downplayed. Sometimes, it is even disqualified that you could have the ability to be compassionate and loving. The role of the nurturer is mostly attributed to women.

However, from creation you were given a huge responsibility to care for creation and not only care for it, but to protect it as well. We clearly see a king's heart to protect when looking at Adam's sacrificial love to defend Eve against the devil. In this modern time, men *are* quite capable of being compassionate and caring. If you don't believe it, consider your passion for sports, cars, and food. Women recognize this capacity when seeing your passion for sports, sometimes to the fault of you crying real tears!

More seriously, great men have demonstrated their passion in positive ways by defending social causes and in fighting social injustices. There is no doubt that Dr. Martin Luther King, Jr. was passionate in fighting against racial discrimination. Another to acknowledge is Mahatma Gandhi, the infamous Eastern Indian activist, who led a nonviolent civil rights movement against the British rule. In fact, Dr. King was greatly impressed and influenced by Gandhi to act on behalf of African Americans. So yes, there is more to you than playing and indulging in pleasures.

Aside from your passion for recreational things, I often wonder what happened throughout the generations of mankind to turn your heart into stone. All over the world mankind has experienced the plight of nations due to a king's callous and cold heart. To be clear, when I refer to "heart" I am not referring to the actual physical organ that enables your blood to circulate through your body. Instead, I am referencing the intangible and invisible capacity to touch and to be touched. It is the spiritual place within you that circulates through your soul and gives you purpose and wholeness.

Your heart first came alive when your Father, God, breathed the breath of life into you and you became a living soul (Genesis 2:7). At is fullest capacity, your heart is the very essence of God. With a properly functioning heart you can conquer anything. It enables you to use your authority wisely with precision and strategy. St. Matthew advised that "***where your treasure is, there will your heart be also,***" **Matthew 6:21**. It is also important to note that from birth the heart is prone to be evil. The prophet Jeremiah provides insight to this: (***The heart is deceitful above***

***all things and desperately wicked, who can know it?* Jeremiah 17:9.** Remember when I shared with you that we were born in sin and formed in iniquity?

For this reason, your heart has to be regenerated or made new otherwise it will be inclined to function in its natural state of sin and hardness. The demise of the heart can be seen on a daily basis when seen in the extreme forms that include murder, child pornography, sex trafficking, drug trafficking, and other crimes against mankind. There is a sign of horror whenever these crimes are mentioned. But, in God's eyes, these sins are no different than lying, stealing, cheating and all of the seemingly, more 'subtle" forms of sin. It is ALL sin.

The Bible strongly proclaims that all have sinned and fallen short of the glory of God. (Romans 3:23) I cannot move forward without encouraging you that if you have been guilty of these crimes that there is forgiveness and redemption for you. It is not impossible to receive forgiveness and salvation. You can find forgiveness after repenting and being Godly sorry for your sins. I will share with you later how you can receive this amazing love if you have not already experienced it.

The reality is that without experiencing God's heart, it is impossible for a king to love and conquer at its highest capacity. IT JUST CANNOT BE DONE! Known to be the wisest man to live, King Solomon, said it best:

"My son, forget not my law; but let thine heart keep my commandments:
2 For length of days, and long life, and peace, shall they add to thee.
3 Let not mercy and truth forsake thee: bind them about thy neck; write them upon the table of thine heart:

4 So shalt thou find favour and good understanding in the sight of God and man.
5 Trust in the Lord with all thine heart; and lean not unto thine own understanding." Proverbs 3:5.

The heart has the ability to protect, love, and conquer. Ironically and sadly, if you do not protect the heart, destruction and despair is inevitable. In my opinion, there is nothing worse than seeing a great man succumb to having his own heart broken. This happens when a king's heart is not properly guarded.

The story of Samson and Delilah is a vivid example of this. Samson was a mighty and strong warrior in the Bible. He had a long track record of defeating Israel's enemies. However, as strong as he was physically, he was weak emotionally. Samson was tricked by the lovely Delilah to discover his source of physical strength. Delilah was hired by Samson's enemies to learn why Samson had never been defeated. While lying in Delilah's lap (somewhere he shouldn't have been), Samson exposed that the secret of his success lied in him not cutting his hair and because of this, he was undefeatable. As a result of him *"letting his hair down"* and letting down his guard, the Philistines attacked him and gouged out his eyes. His betrayal and defeat was a result of his displaced heart. **Proverbs 4:23** advises: *"Keep (guard, watch) your heart with all diligence, for out of it spring the issues of life."*

Just in case it is not clear, please be mindful and intentional about protecting your heart.

Unforgiveness is another major cause of having an unhealthy heart. Sometimes it is more expected for women to hold grudges and be slow to forgive. Interestingly, men can be just as guilty of putting up walls and not allowing love to abide in their hearts. In my observation and experience, I have witnessed men shut off friends and family members from their lives and decide to live in isolation. Instead of practicing good communication skills and clearing up a disagreement, they retreat to live in the silence of pain and hurt. Now this is a real "man cave". It is there that you isolate yourself and shut down. However, no matter how decked out it is, this man cave is not healthy for you or for those who love you.

Even worse, because of the common stereotype that says that strong men are forbidden to be emotional, you have trained yourself to repress your feelings. As a young boy you may have been forced to stop crying after a fall. Not having a moment to recover, you were forced to get up, wipe off the dirt, and to "keep it moving" as if the fall never happened. Right at that instant you were conditioned to believe that your feelings were not appreciated, validated, or wanted.

On the contrary, your female counterparts were coddled and comforted. So, very early you learned that it was not socially acceptable to be emotional or to be comforted in healthy ways. In my point of view, our western world society has created emotionally inept and incompetent men. We have sent dangerous messages to men that being "in touch" with their feelings equate to you being less of a man; and to the very extreme labeled as effeminate or gay.

Clearly, this is not true. Some of the strongest men in the Bible were physically *and* emotionally strong. King David is a significant and powerful example of this truth. Maybe he would have been compared to Michael Jordan or Tiger Woods when it comes to confidence and skill. While he was smaller in stature compared to Goliath, he was a mighty man of war. His confidence transcended the norm. Really, can you imagine an estimated 6 foot tall boy killing a 9 foot giant? As confident and courageous as he was, King David still was capable of sharing his deepest fears with God. His transparency did not emasculate

him, instead it was his humanistic and passionate characteristics that made him great. King David had favor with God. In **Psalm 17:8**, he bragged about being "the apple of God's eye".

King David showed that intimacy was appropriate and acceptable. Not only with Bathsheba, but with God as well.

Today, nearly 75 of the 150 Psalms are attributed to him. In them, you will see a very real span of a man's emotions and his ability to be vulnerable. King David expressed feelings of defeat, insecurity, hopelessness, rejection and fear. Did this make him weak? No, far from it. This demonstrated his ability to be open in sharing the matters of his heart to a loving and caring God. In return of him sharing his heart with God, he was empowered and enabled to do the extraordinary.

He accomplished what no other King had done. The openness of his inadequacies continue to inspire and comfort millions and billions of people all over the world! I suggest that his humility was stronger than his ability to kill Goliath. Do you wonder what extraordinary things you are capable of fulfilling if you become transparent with God?

Personally, I do not know how my own walk with the Lord would be without having the Psalms for comfort, courage, and strength. I have so many "favorites" that it is hard to choose just one. In moments of weakness, I will say that **Psalm 55** has to be top on the list when I am uncertain, experiencing anxiety and in need of defense:

"Give ear to my prayer, O God; and hide not thyself from my supplication.
2 Attend unto me, and hear me: I mourn in my complaint, and make a noise;
3 Because of the voice of the enemy, because of the oppression of the wicked: for they cast iniquity upon me, and in wrath they hate me.
4 My heart is sore pained within me: and the terrors of death are fallen upon me.
5 Fearfulness and trembling are come upon me, and horror hath overwhelmed me.

6 And I said, Oh that I had wings like a dove! for then would I fly away, and be at rest.
7 Lo, then would I wander far off, and remain in the wilderness. Selah.
8 I would hasten my escape from the windy storm and tempest.
9 Destroy, O Lord, and divide their tongues: for I have seen violence and strife in the city.
10 Day and night they go about it upon the walls thereof: mischief also and sorrow are in the midst of it.
11 Wickedness is in the midst thereof: deceit and guile depart not from her streets.
12 For it was not an enemy that reproached me; then I could have borne it: neither was it he that hated me that did magnify himself against me; then I would have hid myself from him:
13 But it was thou, a man mine equal, my guide, and mine acquaintance.
14 We took sweet counsel together, and walked unto the house of God in company.
15 Let death seize upon them, and let them go down quick into hell: for wickedness is in their dwellings, and among them.
16 As for me, I will call upon God; and the Lord shall save me.
17 Evening, and morning, and at noon, will I pray, and cry aloud: and he shall hear my voice.

18 He hath delivered my soul in peace from the battle that was against me: for there were many with me.
19 God shall hear, and afflict them, even he that abideth of old. Selah. Because they have no changes, therefore they fear not God.
20 He hath put forth his hands against such as be at peace with him: he hath broken his covenant.
21 The words of his mouth were smoother than butter, but war was in his heart: his words were softer than oil, yet were they drawn swords.
22 Cast thy burden upon the Lord, and he shall sustain thee: he shall never suffer the righteous to be moved.
23 But thou, O God, shalt bring them down into the pit of destruction: bloody and deceitful men shall not live out half their days; but I will trust in thee."

Another favorite- **Psalm 27:**

"The Lord is my light and my salvation;
Whom shall I fear?
The Lord is the strength of my life;
Of whom shall I be afraid?
2 When the wicked came against me
To eat up my flesh,
My enemies and foes,
They stumbled and fell.
3 Though an army may encamp against me,
My heart shall not fear;
Though war may rise against me,
In this I will be confident.
4 One thing I have desired of the Lord,
That will I seek:

*That I may dwell in the house of the Lord
All the days of my life,
To behold the beauty of the Lord,
And to inquire in His temple.
5 For in the time of trouble
He shall hide me in His pavilion;
In the secret place of His tabernacle
He shall hide me;
He shall set me high upon a rock.
6 And now my head shall be lifted up above my enemies all around me;
Therefore I will offer sacrifices of joy in His tabernacle;
I will sing, yes, I will sing praises to the Lord.
7 Hear, O Lord, when I cry with my voice!
Have mercy also upon me, and answer me.
8 When You said, "Seek My face,"
My heart said to You, "Your face, Lord, I will seek."
9 Do not hide Your face from me;
Do not turn Your servant away in anger;
You have been my help;
Do not leave me nor forsake me,
O God of my salvation.
10 When my father and my mother forsake me,
Then the Lord will take care of me.
11 Teach me Your way, O Lord,
And lead me in a smooth path, because of my enemies.
12 Do not deliver me to the will of my adversaries;
For false witnesses have risen against me,
And such as breathe out violence.
13 I would have lost heart, unless I had believed
That I would see the goodness of the Lord*

In the land of the living.
14 Wait on the Lord;
Be of good courage,
And He shall strengthen your heart;
Wait, I say, on the Lord!"

King, I know that you have been tirelessly working to be what everyone else thinks you should be. You have worked hard to look the role and play the part. Some of you have done all of the "right" things. You've worked hard, established a thick bank roll, made the right investments, purchased the house in the right neighborhood, sent your children to private schools...and the list goes on and on. In spite of all of these accomplishments, have you done the work on your heart?

Have you invested in things that matter the most? Is your heart right with God? Is your wife happy and fulfilled? Does she respect and honor you? Have you even committed yourself to one woman and only exchanged with covenant lips? Or, are you spreading your royal seed across the land? Are you taking responsibility and raising your seed? Do your children enjoy spending time with you? Are you establishing a legacy for them?

Do your friends trust and believe in you? Are you making a difference in your community, or are you apathetic in thinking that social change is someone else's job? While it could appear that you are on the "right" track, what does God think?

"But the LORD said unto Samuel, Look not on his countenance, or on the height of his stature; because I have refused him: for the LORD seeth not as man seeth;

for man looketh on the outward appearance, but the LORD looketh on the heart." **I Samuel 16:7**

What I really desire for you to know is that your heart has the capacity to be passionate, compassionate, and loving. These attributes do not imply that you are weak or any less of a man. Likewise, it is vital that you work hard to protect your heart. Do not be distracted like Samson and allow anyone or anything to destroy your heart and ultimately hinder your destiny.

Most importantly, having an open and transparent relationship with your creator, Father God, will result in your ruling and reigning as king in your life. This will occur when He has complete reign of your heart. *"The king's heart is in the hand of the Lord, as the rivers of water: he turneth it whithersoever he will."* **Proverbs 21:1**

Dear Father God,

First, I greatly appreciate your love. You are the supreme example of love because You *ARE* love. You were a mastermind when creating man to have the capacity to love and to be loved. My prayer is that you would touch the heart of every man reading these pages. When they are insecure in demonstrating their true feelings, may they find a safe place in you to be open and transparent. Let them know that they can trust you and that you will not betray them, no matter how hurtful or severe the matter may be.

Download your strength and power each time they call upon you. Please give them wisdom as they connect with others. Allow them to see the benefits of having a relationship with you as their relationships with others become stronger and healthier. Father, I rebuke the devourer that seeks to defeat and to destroy them through the matters of their heart.
In its place, I pronounce a release of love, comfort, security, and confidence to take root and remain there. In Jesus Christ's Name, amen.

Chapter 5
ALL THE KING'S HORSES

Dear Your Highness,

Have you ever had a dream that you were being chased? In that dream, did it seem like the chase would never end? In fact, you probably woke up in a sweat before the chase ended! This has happened to me before and I remember being in terror as my heart was racing and feeling like there was no hope. Actually, it was a relief to wake up because at least then, the chase was over.

Since Adam, Satan has had an agenda to destroy you by chasing you. He is that invisible enemy chasing you in the dream. Although that may have been a dream for you, the reality is that there is a ferocious devil chasing you. Satan's goal is to keep you running aimlessly, eventually to your demise. In **Peter 5:8 (NKJV)** it is explained like this:

"Your adversary the devil walks about like a roaring lion, seeking whom he may devour."

Again this chase is not new. It is Satan's retaliation from being demoted from his high status as a chief angel. His arrogance and pride caused him to desire to be God. God is very clear that there is only ONE God and that there was no room to share. At that point, Satan was cast out of heaven. Breaking news: Satan hates you! *"**The thief cometh not, but for to steal, and to kill, and to destroy."** St John 10:10 a.*

To further explain this, imagine yourself on foot and being chased by an army of horses. Realistically, there is no way that you could survive this chase. The horses are stronger and faster. Eventually, you will be trampled upon and mauled by the horses. This reminds me of the story of the children of Israel

being chased by Pharaoh. The nation of Israel was God's people. The other nations were pagan and served various other gods. Pharaoh, the king of Egypt, hated the nation of Israel and they became slaves to Pharaoh. Israel served Pharaoh in Egypt close to 400 years.

However, God raised up a "king" in Moses to lead Israel out of Egypt. When God spoke to Moses to lead the people out of bondage, Pharaoh used 600 chariots to chase Israel. All of the odds-all 600 of them, were against Israel who ran by foot. Pharaoh's army was physically greater, stronger, and mightier. Israel's success could only be accomplished by obeying God's instructions.

As the miraculous story ends, Moses and Israel crossed the parted Red Sea onto dry ground. This was the same Red Sea that swallowed up Pharaoh and his 600 chariots. That ended the chase for Pharaoh's army, but unfortunately not for Israel. In the book of Numbers, it shows where they would go on to suffer in the wilderness 40 years because their heart was hardened. Like discussed in chapter four, this is a vivid reminder to conquer the matters of your heart, before they conquer you.

Today, it will take obedience to God's word to put the chase in your life to a halt. This will prevent you from running in circles and being enslaved to sin. To Israel, the chaser was Satan disguised as Pharaoh. For you, it could be Satan disguised through a variety of vices. Ultimately, the goal is to keep you running from your destiny.

There is nothing more disturbing than to see kings being chased by infidelity, pride, lying, greed, and so many other forms of corruption. What really blows my mind is that these same, old vices have chased men for many generations. It is often said that Satan does not need to use any new weapons to destroy people because the age-old weapons continue to work.

The Bible says it best:

"That which has been is what will be. That which is done is what will be done, and there is nothing new under the sun." (Ecclesiastes 1:9 NKJV)

Really, why would anyone try something new when what you have been using continues to work?

For centuries, kingdoms and nations have been destroyed by a man's pride, greed, hatred, and sexual immorality. Even still, we see major public figures, politicians, and great leader's demise in exchange for 20 minutes of sexual pleasure that leaves a lifetime of pain and humiliation.

Most recently, the world has lost and continues to lose gifted and talented celebrities to substance abuse and suicide even though, they saw the same vices destroy their colleagues. Outside of the glitz and cameras, the chase is the same for regular, everyday people. Sin is universal and it does not discriminate!

News flash: the chase *IS* real! It is time for you to take inventory of your life. What is chasing you? What is keeping you from reigning in your life as the king you were created to be? Is it pornography, adultery, or drug and alcohol use? Is it greed or the desire to be so successful that you are a workaholic and that keeps you running? Have you abandoned your family and broken the hearts of your wife and children? The list could go on, but as you read this book, you can answer this for yourself.

Ironically, something I found amazing is that one of the ways to end the chase, is to run-yes, **RUN**! *"**Flee also youthful lusts: but follow righteousness, faith, charity, peace, with them that call on the Lord out of a pure heart."* **2 Timothy 2:22**

Ultimately, God never intended for you to be chased by sin. In **James 4:7 (NKJV)**, you are encouraged to submit to God, to resist the devil and he will flee from you! This will only

work if you first submit yourself to God. Then, after being empowered with God's spirit, there are moments where you will run a different race by fleeing from the sin. When striving for your crown, Apostle Paul brilliantly says it best:

"Do you not know that those who run in a race all run, but one receives the prize? Run in such a way that you may obtain it (crown). And everyone who competes for the prize is temperate in all things. Now they do it to obtain a perishable crown, but we for an imperishable crown. Therefore I run thus: not with uncertainty. Thus I fight: not as one who beats the air. But I discipline my body and bring it into subjection, lest, when I have preached to others, I myself should become disqualified." I Corinthians 9:24. Basically, Paul shared with us his strategy for success. He disciplined himself to win by denying himself from immorality."

Another source of empowerment can be found in **Hebrews 12:1 (NKJV)** which states:

"Therefore we also, since we are surrounded by so great a cloud of witnesses, let us lay aside every weight, and the sin which so easily

ensnares us, let us run with endurance the race that is set before us."

Finally, I want you to be very clear that there is a chase on your life. The 600 horses and chariots may not be coming for you, but the impact of what is chasing you is just as powerful. In order to win and to rule in your life, you will need to be empowered by God's spirit. This will enable you to resist the devil and in return you will chase what has been chasing you!

Dear Heavenly Father,

Thank you for providing your kings with the revelation of Satan's agenda to destroy them through the chase. With your Spirit, help them to see the places of defeat in their lives. Help them to realize that these sins continue to rob them of their birthright to reign as king. Even now, I am praying that you will convict them by your Holy Spirit and that the pleasure they once felt will no longer remain. Lord, do not allow them to continue in the vicious cycle, but free them to live fulfilled and victorious lives.

As a result they will continue to build in the kingdom instead of destroying kingdoms. Also, please bring restoration and healing to those who have been hurt and broken as a result of their indiscretions. I pray the latter part of St. John 10:10 over their lives right now, that they will have life more abundantly because this is the essence of why you came to save! In your precious and mighty name, Jesus Christ, amen.

Chapter 6
ALL THE KING'S MEN

Dear Your Highness,

You are strong, powerful, and courageous. Can I ask, "Where is your tribe?" Who is in your court, your royal court that is? In other words, who are your supporters? Who has your back? Who is watching out for you? Can you identify these people in your life?

All successful kings have a royal court. In royalty, there exists several protocols or official ways of doing things. Having the right people in your court ensures a proper reign.

In the beginning, God established that it is not good for you to be alone (Genesis 2:18). Mankind was created to live together and to do life together. A fulfilled life is that of sharing your journey with the people you love and those who love you.

The institution of family was created by God and it was intended to reflect His love for us.

I would argue that in contrast, a king who is isolated and alone cannot properly have dominion in his life. Without healthy relationships, there is not any substance in which to measure your dominion. It is not only crucial that you share your life with others, but it is equally important *who* shares your life. Maybe before now you were not as discriminating in who was allowed into your royal court. This can happen when you allow toxic people into your inner circle.

Personally, there is something so unattractive about a man who is a follower and who is easily influenced by others. What kind of king is he if he cannot make decisions for himself? That's not a monarchy that is evidence of a democracy and God created you to rule your kingdom, not someone else. It's a sad
sight to see grown men making poor choices because their associates have influenced or provoked them to do so. These toxic relationships eventually end in devastation.

Then, there are family relationships where you did not have the privilege to choose who to let into your court. Often family relationships can zap all of the vitality and joy from your life if you allow it.

I recommend that you take inventory of the people in your life to maximize and receive the most benefits from those relationships. Are you constantly investing more energy, time, and resources in relationships than you are receiving? If so, this is not healthy for you or for them. Those on the receiving end are being enabled and they are not living up to their highest potential. The longer you enable them, the less likely they will become independent. In your evaluation, be mindful to identify the relationships that should be cultivated, maintained, or eliminated.

To elaborate, the court is a formal word for household or entourage. I have estimated that your court should include at least a couple of these or all of these kinds of people: ***Comrade/Companion, Advisor, Guardian, and/or an Aide***.

In your mind, a ***Comrade*** may be better understood as a "buddy" or "homie". The comrade is a companion who provides you unconditional love and fun. It could be a childhood friend, a college friend, or one who has fulfilled that role in your adulthood. You get the idea- this relationship is really organic and easy. This is where you can "let your hair down" and just be you. Having this level of relationship is so necessary. With your buddy, you do not need to explain yourself all of the time. They just get you. They laugh at your corny jokes and your ridiculous ways of doing things.

Envision how you feel when attending a sports event or hanging out at the barbershop for a couple of hours, even *after* you have already been serviced. While so many other relationships can be draining, the friendship of a comrade "fills your tank" and can be very fulfilling. I love how "Wise Solomon" puts it:

"There are "friends" who destroy each other, but a real friend sticks closer than a brother." Proverbs 18:24, NLT.

In a busy world, it may not be realistic to spend your entire time with a comrade. I doubt that your family or employers would appreciate that. Still, be intentional about fostering and maintaining those healthy relationships. Spending just the right time with your buddy will result in happy spouses, children, and employers because of the fulfillment it gives you.

Perhaps you need a comrade in your life and there isn't one. Have you worked so hard to be successful that you have neglected your friendships? My encouragement is that you get connected and in some cases, reconnected. Do not live this life alone. There are several ways to establish a comrade friendship. Your church may have recreational activities, a Men's Bible Study, or a small group where you can get connected. Joining a sports league is another great way to meet friends.

Another positive way to locate a comrade could be by volunteering your time in community service. Goodness can be like a magnet. When you are doing good things, you will attract good people to your entourage. Providing acts of service is something very dear to my heart. For me, there is no better feeling than making a difference in someone else's life. Your community could greatly benefit from your selfless acts of kindness. The bottom line: get connected and enjoy the simple friendship of a comrade.

Next, a king must have an *Advisor* in their court. This can be portrayed in the form of a trusted mentor. The qualities of an advisor include one who has advanced knowledge and skills that will improve and enhance your life. Good advisors are wise, trustworthy, and dependable. Often they can be accountability partners who you can confide your deepest failures, struggles, and disappointments. This is not to condone your sinful acts or enable you to continue down the wrong path.

On the contrary-they exhibit strengths in areas that will cause you to rise above your circumstances. This is a very important need. One who is isolated and experiencing secret struggles will more than likely remain defeated.

James 5:16:

"Confess your faults one to another, and pray one for another, that ye may be healed. The effectual fervent prayer of a righteous man availeth much."

Advisors are not your competitor and their whole purpose is to coach you into success. In fact, you may be more inclined to see them as a coach. Their expertise and proven track record could enhance your life in areas of health, finances, career, and relationships.

Proverbs 15:22 (NLT) says it beautifully: ***"Plans go wrong for lack of advice; many advisers bring success."***

Something to consider: you may be doing fine now however, how much more could you excel if you had a trusted advisor in your life? Plainly, sometimes you need a "Nathan" in your life like King David had. Nathan warned and exposed King David when he sinned. Nathan was an accountability partner and an advisor. Without a Nathan in his life, King David would have eventually been demoted from his position. God hates sin and it would have destroyed him and ultimately it would have altered his reign over God's children.

When God provides you a Nathan-like advisor, do not shun or avoid him. This help is actually evidence of God's love for you and His strong desire for you to succeed. ***"For the LORD disciplines those he*** *loves, and he punishes each one he accepts as his child."* **Hebrews 12:6 (NLT).**

A complete and well run court also needs a ***Guardian*** or bodyguard. Before I lose you to this idea, I realize that unless you are a celebrity, you will less likely be walking around with a bodyguard. It would be quite comical for you to show up at work with "detail". Instead, I am referring to you having a person in your life who is a protector and has your physical, mental, and emotional safety as their top priority. Basically, guardians have your back. Celebrities are not the only ones who need guardians in their life.

For those who are married, your wife is the ***best*** guardian possible. While you are her kingly covering, a Godly wife will cover you in prayer. There are not many things as powerful as a praying wife to intercede on your behalf. If you really want to reap the benefits of a praying wife, treat her like a queen and there is nothing she will not do for you!!! Go ahead and try it, you will not be sorry.

Lastly, having an ***Aide*** in your reach is essential. This is a helper who finds it natural to assist you in times of need. You can count on this person to lend a hand without "payback" or any strings attached. Anyone who has ulterior motives is not the best person to serve in this role.

To further explain, who do you call when you need extra hands to move or who in your life has a pickup truck when you need to move? When you have a flat tire and there is not roadside assistance, who can give you a lift? Who is willing to take you to the airport when you want to avoid paying astronomical parking fees? Again, married men should expect their wives to be first to fulfill these roles if they are appropriate and realistic for them and if the wife does not mind. Your wife was created to be your helper. ***"And the LORD God said, It is not good that the man should be alone; I will make him an help meet for him."* Genesis 2:18.**
Today, there are women who change tires and drive pickup trucks. Personally, I have no desire to do it, but I believe that I could, if necessary. Like me, there are other wives who would be more than willing to help their husbands. These can be great bonding opportunities and ways to deepen your relationship.

Playing it safe, you would be wise to enlist your queen as the first choice in all of these roles. This will provide a safe and enforced kingdom.

With too many others involved, you risk the possibility of being "chased" and tempted to sin. There is still room to include others in your circle, but be smart and careful in your choosing.

Now, I feel like the Surgeon General when I warn you that it is very unreasonable to expect anyone to be 100% reliable. We are all human and we are all subject to failing at some point. Our complete reliance should be in our Lord, Jesus Christ. He is our true protector and defense.

Still, having one or two people in your life who can fulfill any or all of these roles of **Comrade, Advisor, Guardian, and Aide**, will provide you a balanced and well-functioning life. Ultimately, with God and the service of your court, you will be fully equipped to reign!

Speaking about romantic relationships is always interesting and a challenge. Yet, it is a vital component of a man's life. Again, a king needs a kingdom. In your kingdom, you were created to share your life with your "Eve", your queen, but it is essential that your queen is of equal integrity, virtue, and excellence. ***"Do not waste your strength on women, on those who ruin kings."*** **Proverbs 31:3a NLT Also**, you do not want a woman tearing down your kingdom. ***"The wise woman builds her house, But the foolish tears it down with her own hands."*** **Proverbs 14:1.** A special note: a Godly woman wants to share her life with a Godly man. So, if you are still trying to be "Rico Suave" or a player, stop looking for the "good thing". *"**Whoever finds a wife finds a good thing, and obtains favor of the LORD."* **Proverbs 18:22.** Just wait until you are ready, this will save everyone precious time.

In your search for a wife, the Bible warns against a couple being unequally yoked. ***"Be ye not unequally yoked together with unbelievers: for what fellowship hath righteousness with unrighteousness? And what communion hath light with darkness?"* 2 Corinthians 6:14.** Plainly, you need a good match in order to reign. Today, the matchmaking industry is a billion dollar business.

I am not interested in the debate whether or not a Christian should use these services to find their future husband or wife. Allow the Holy Spirit to guide you.
Although, when you rely on Him alone, He will provide you with the best mate for you and for *free*! God's ways are always the best. Something else to consider: the idea that just because you both are "believers" or "saved" is **not** enough. When God created the earth, he provided an abundance of delightful things for us to enjoy. In His creation, flowers come in all sorts

of colors, there are innumerable animals, and so many wonderful fruits and vegetables. With this in mind, do not settle! God has a perfect fit for *you*! Your queen may not be perfect, but she will perfectly compliment you.

Another warning, please do yourself and the young lady a favor. Do away with the games and shenanigans. Once more, no one has time for disrespect and the wasting of their precious time. A real king is decisive and direct. A woman loves a man who knows what they want and they do whatever it takes to get it. That would be a good time for you to *"**chase**"* as opposed to you getting chased as discussed in Chapter 5. A king uses his power properly and has good intentions.

Today, many women worry that there are not enough men to go around. Sometimes, it seems like the women outweigh the amount of single, heterosexual, Christian, men. If you meet these qualifications, please do not take advantage of a lady's feelings. Looking out for all of my Virtuous Sisters: if you do not have plans of building a future with her, *MOVE ON*! Life is too short, and they are too precious to God for you to misuse and abuse them.

There is a spiritual law that says that you will reap what you sow. *"**Be not deceived; God is not mocked: for whatsoever a man soweth, that shall he also reap.**"*
Galatians 6:7. In other words, the disrespect that you give, is what will come back to you. Your inconsideration will reverse and hurt you. To sum

it up, if you would like to have a Proverbs 31 Woman, then present yourself to her as a *Proverbs 31 Man*!

Dear Heavenly Father,

It is refreshing to know that you never intended for your children to do life alone. You promised us that you would never leave us or forsake us. It is because of your care that you have provided us with the capacity to share our lives with others. Father, please provide wisdom to your kings so that they will be able to determine the difference between healthy and toxic relationships.

If there is one who is isolated and feeling alone, please surround them with friends and advisors who will help them along their journey. Also, raise up a "Nathan" and supply them with honorable and respectable men in their lives who will hold them accountable. If by chance they have disrespected women in the past, please forgive them and equip them to be Godly men again. When they have presented themselves worthy, connect them to their queen and bless their union. Let it be the model of your love for all people. In Jesus Christ's Name, amen.

MY ROYAL COURT

Use this tool to take inventory of your court.

My Comrade(s): _____

My Advisor(s): _____

My Guardian(s): _____

My Aide(s): _____

Chapter 7
"KING ME"

Now, it is the time to share with you all of your benefits of serving as a king in the Kingdom of God. In the beginning, I shared with you that you were born to reign as king. From creation it was God's plan all along for you to rule and have dominion in your kingdom (life). In my observation, I have seen your anguish and desire to shirk your responsibility to rule.

Never in this entire book did I imply that being a king was an easy task. Sometimes, men *do* have it hard. There are a lot of expectations for you to meet. At times, it may seem that the demands on you to perform can be unbearable. Not only are you challenged to perform, but in many cases you are expected to over perform, all because you are a man.

Sometimes, society sends confusing messages where we expect you to be hard and strong. But in relationships, it is desired for you to be loving and understanding. At times you may feel that you cannot win for losing. Good news: you *can* win, you *can* reign and rule as king.

Spiritually speaking, you were set up to win. God would never create you to be king and not provide you the tools and resources to fulfil this demanding role. Having a relationship with God and using the best strategy ever, His spirit, will empower you to successfully accomplish this challenge.

Here is where I share details about your coronation. In actual monarchies, when a prince is born, it is inevitable that one day he will be king. From birth he is groomed to wear a crown. In actuality, the prince is already a king just waiting to happen.

The same is true for you. Just like the Prophet Jeremiah, your destiny was determined before you were formed in your mother's womb. **"Before I formed you in the womb I knew you, And before you were born I consecrated you; I have appointed you a prophet to the nations." Jeremiah 1:5 NASB** Until now, you may have been living as the prince, not stepping up to the challenge and avoiding your kingly duties. This is where I am reminded of King David. He was chosen to be a king as a boy, but was not coronated right away. You see, he had to kill a lion, a bear, and a giant before he could be trusted in his predestined role.

What in your life do you need to kill? Whatever it is, the moment that it is annihilated, the sooner you will be allowed to wear your crown. The challenges, temptations, and obstacles are strategically allowed by God to groom and prepare you. As a result, you are equipped and empowered to advance to the next level of royalty. Challenges also develop discipline and integrity in you. King David said it like this:

"It is good for me that I have been afflicted; that I might learn thy statutes." Psalm 119:71

The reality is that you will not be ready to reign until you experience challenges and hardships. No one is exempt from this. These same challenges can create a new and deeper relationship between you and God. Who better to help you live as a king than the KING of KINGS?

The significance of your coronation is that it is the official verification that your status has changed from prince to king. Jesus Christ himself was coronated. Do you remember when the dove rested on him after He was baptized? Even more extraordinary, was when He was given a crown of thorns at the crucifixion. Even Jesus Christ himself, the King of all Kings, was crowned. Although He was born a king, He endured a bloody cross for all of our sins. His resurrection was the coronation and without it, none of us would have access to His kingdom.

Similarly, your coronation takes place when you are baptized into Jesus Christ. Because of Adam's failure, the original plan to live as king was altered and delayed. Being born again frees you from sin because you have the nature of your Heavenly Father and not your natural father. When the King of Kings was crowned Lord of Lords, His shed blood made it possible for you to be restored back to the original plan of supremacy and dominion.

"And almost all things are by the law purged with blood; and without shedding of blood is no remission." Hebrews 9:22

The fact is that you cannot properly rule or reign if you are in the same state as the fallen Adam. The culmination takes place when you have recognized your sins, repented, and have been made new through the baptism of the water and Spirit.

"Jesus answered and said unto him, Verily, verily, I say unto thee, Except a man be born again, he cannot see the kingdom of God." St. John 3:3

Just in case you believe that you are the biggest sinner in the world and that there is nothing that can save you, this is farthest from the truth. Jesus Christ came especially for you!

As a new creation, you are now ready to be robed in royalty as a follower of Christ. This is when you have acknowledged God as King and as a result, you have given Him permission to rule and reign in your heart. Having the Holy Spirit empowers you to defeat sin, to love like Him and to overcome life's struggles.

What was extremely difficult in your life before, now will be possible for you to overcome. It also provides a Comforter that forever lives in your heart. Jesus Christ is the very best friend that you can have and no one else can comfort you like Him!

Another benefit is being adopted into a huge family of fellow believers. You will no longer be considered a stranger to

God, because you are His son. ***"Beloved, now are we the sons of God, and it doth not yet appear what we shall be: but we know that, when he shall appear, we shall be like him; for we shall see him as he is."*** **I John 3:2.** Having Jesus Christ as your father, you have a defender who will fight for you. In fact you already have the victory as His child. ***"But thanks be to God, who gives us the victory through our Lord Jesus Christ."*** **I Corinthians 15:58.** The bottom line is that you are a winner.

As if the other benefits were not enough, not only will God provide for you, but He has given you the power to get wealth. ***"But you shall*** *remember the LORD your God: for it is he that gives you power to get wealth that he may establish his covenant which he swore unto your fathers, as it is this day."* **Deuteronomy 8:18.** You see, God is concerned about every aspect of your life.

If you are really ready to reign, there are extraordinary abilities that you are offered.

***"Now unto him that is able to do exceeding abundantly above all that we ask or think, according to the power that worketh in us,* Ephesians 3:20.** Some of these privileges include healing the sick. ***"They shall take up serpents; and if they drink any deadly thing, it shall not hurt them; they shall lay hands on the sick, and they shall recover."* Mark 16:18.**

It is this same power that can be used to resist the temptation that has been defeating you for too long. This is the power of faith. Do you believe this, I mean do you really believe this? I want you to know that it *is* real. I have witnessed so many miracles in my life and I am convinced that God's power is real. It's amazing to me of how Christians get a bad rap for having faith and believing in the supernatural.

Rarely are witchdoctors and voodoo followers questioned and God's power supersedes any other power.

Hopefully, you have a new perspective of who you are and that you do not have to live a dull and powerless life. Instead, you can live with power and authority. Unlike the superficial and temporary power of the world, this power is everlasting and eternal. You see, Barack Obama will soon lose his power as President when the next one is inaugurated. In God's kingdom, you can have favor (power) with Him and man.

"So shalt thou find favour and good understanding in the sight of God and man." **Proverbs 3:4**

In addition to all of these wonderful benefits, you will be in fellowship with God again because your relationship with Him will no longer severed. Because God hates sin, a plan to redeem us back was necessary. Now, you can connect with God
in confidence because sin no longer is in the way. It is important to know that even after your initial salvation, it is necessary to keep a clear connection with God. As I stated before, God will advocate for you if you sin, after you have confessed and repented. But, do not allow ongoing sin

to separate you from your Father again. *"What shall we say then? Shall we continue in sin, that grace may abound? God forbid. How shall we, that are dead to sin, live any longer therein?"* **Romans 6:1-2.**

In the workplace, each employee has a preference as to which benefit is the best for them. Some think it's the health benefits. However, if your spouse has a better plan, accepting insurance on your job will not be as valuable. For you, the matching 401k may take precedence because you are really strategic about planning for your children's college education or for your retirement. In the Kingdom of God, there is no question which is the best benefit of all. Absolutely, it is living eternally with Jesus Christ in Heaven when He returns. When I was young, I remember hearing about going to heaven all of the time. Sadly, today we do not talk about it enough. Looking at the signs of the times, Jesus is so very soon to return.

If you have been born again with water baptism and been filled with His Spirit, you will go with Him when He returns.

"Jesus answered, Verily, verily, I say unto thee, Except a man be born of water and of the Spirit, he cannot enter into the kingdom of God." **St. John 3:5**

And the happy ending to this story:

"But I would not have you to be ignorant, brethren, concerning them which are asleep, that ye sorrow not, even as others which have no hope. 14 For if we believe that Jesus died and rose again, even so them also which sleep in Jesus will God bring with him. 15 For this we say unto you by the word of the Lord, that we which are alive and remain unto the coming of the Lord shall not prevent them which are asleep. 16 For the Lord himself shall

descend from heaven with a shout, with the voice of the archangel, and with the trump of God: and the dead in Christ shall rise first: 17 Then we which are alive and remain shall be caught up together with them in the clouds, to meet the Lord in the air: and so shall we ever be with the Lord. 18 Wherefore comfort one another with these words." **I Thessalonians 4:13-18**

Whether you like it or not, no one will live on this earth forever. Earth as we know it will pass away and we all will live somewhere, eternally. Would prefer to live with Jesus Christ, or would you prefer to live with Satan? You see, the ultimate plan for you to reign is not just for your life here on earth. On the contrary, God really designed your life to live forever with Him. Together, you will reign in Heaven.

Dear Heavenly Father,

I am so excited for all of the kings who have chosen to learn more about their identity in you. Although society would like to dictate what a man should be or look like, it is your plan that truly gives men peace, balance, and completeness. Now, Father, I am praying that each king who has read this book will be touched and their lives forever changed. Open their eyes to see the majestic master plan that you have for them. They all come from different walks of life, backgrounds, and cultures.

However, your love is universal and transcends them all. If they have not yet given you permission to be King over their life, will you lead them to a faith community that will mentor and support them in their journey?

After they have accepted salvation, please allow your love to radiate in every facet of their life. Give them wisdom conquer financially and in return they will support your
ministry with their added resources. Mend any broken marriages and heal relationships with their children. Destroy the bondage of sexual

immorality and restore integrity and righteousness into their lives. Enable them to flee youthful lusts and to not fall to temptations. Give them a desire to accept their responsibilities. Remind them to guard their hearts and to engage in only healthy and positive relationships.

When being beat down from the world and its pleasures, please replenish their self-esteem and self-worth. Reveal to them that they are the "head and not the tail" and that they are "above and not beneath". Give them a hunger and thirst for your righteousness. Please lead them to their special assignment of service in the Kingdom of God, as they continue to walk with you. Allow them to make a positive impact in their communities and cause their dominion to attract more kings for the kingdom. Until the final coronation of your coming, keep

them in your loving care and provision. In Jesus Christ's Name, amen.

FINAL WORDS

It has been a privilege to share with you my newly found admiration and appreciation for God's wonderful creation, men. Writing this book has been therapeutic and healing for me and I pray the same will happen for all who read these pages. Ultimately, God was not confused when He created men and women. His plan for us all is to reign and have dominion in our lives. In order for this to take place, we have to know our identity and who we are in Christ.

Men's value and worth is not to be downplayed or devalued. In the past 2 years, the United States has witnessed a surge of brutish and evil crimes against men, specifically African American men. The unsubstantiated killings of African American men is an epidemic. This is a spiritual battle that can only be fought and won with God's spirit. Never has it been more imperative that the faith community bind together in love and fight back in these injustices to **all** mankind. Let's fight for our kings by using the most powerful weapon to exist, **God's Love!**

THOUGHTS & IDEAS

THOUGHTS & IDEAS

MEET THE AUTHOR

Nicole Young Starks is the Founder of *Victorious by Design, International* and *Victoriously, Nicole!* *Victorious by Design, International* is a Global Women's Outreach Ministry designed to actualize the fullest potential in women. Programs and services provided include: women's fellowship opportunities, community volunteer services, informative workshops, refreshing retreats, and exhilarating conferences. In collaboration with Convoy of Hope and Heartland Church, Nicole expanded her global impact by experiencing her first mission trip to Haiti in 2015. In 2016, she has plans to serve again, this time in South Africa.

Victoriously, Nicole! is the up close and personal component of Nicole's mission. Through this, Nicole demonstrates her gift to encourage, inspire, and motivate.

As a *"faith coach"*, she provides one on one coaching to those who have been stuck in various parts of their lives.

Her personal testimony of overcoming and being victorious is the force behind her mission. Just as she is passionate and determined, she is equally compassionate and empathetic. Her very personal walk with Jesus Christ empowers her to share His love with others, whether it be through word or deed.

Although she has spent nearly 20 years in career and ministry serving women and children, most recently she was inspired to speak to men. Her belief is that when men are empowered to live their best lives, inevitably the women will follow.

Nicole constantly strives to answer a calling to lead others into "Victorious Living". An ordained minister, chaplain, counselor, public speaker, songwriter, event coordinator, mentor, coach, and conference host...she never tires of finding a platform to serve God and his people.

With a practical and real approach, she is gifted to impact others from all walks of life. Her greatest joy is to see others succeed and to win! She proclaims that *"life is to be lived and not endured or tolerated."*

REFERENCES

All biblical scripture references were retrieved from the King James Version, unless otherwise stated.

www.ingramcontent.com/pod-product-compliance
Lightning Source LLC
Chambersburg PA
CBHW050654160426
43194CB00010B/1936